Chimps Can Be Chums

By Liza Charlesworth

ISBN: 978-1-339-02770-8

Art Director: Tannaz Fassihi; Designer: Tanya Chernyak
Photos © Getty Images.

1 2 3 4 5 6 7 8 9 10   68   32 31 30 29 28 27 26 25 24 23
Printed in Jiaxing, China. First printing, August 2023.

■SCHOLASTIC

It's a chimp and a chimp.
Chimps can be chums!

A chimp can stand on 2 legs.
But it runs on 4 limbs.

A chimp is a champ!
It can grip a branch.
It can run as fast as a man.

Chimps munch plants and nuts.
Chimps chomp eggs and bugs.

Chimps can do so much!
A chimp can dig with a stick.
It can chop with a rock.

See the chimp on its mom's back.
The chimp gets a lift
so it can rest.

It's a chimp, a chimp, and a chimp.
Chimps can be chums.
They can chill!